The Dawlish Co[...]

Bernard Chapm[an]

OBELISK PUBLICATIONS

PLATE ACKNOWLEDGEMENTS

It is an impossible task for me to pinpoint the precise origin of every photograph in this book. I would therefore like to thank all those people who have kindly supplied me with pictures in the past. Hopefully they will be able to share the pleasure of showing some of Dawlish's past in this photographic presentation.

Other Obelisk Publications

AROUND & ABOUT THE HALDON HILLS, Chips Barber
THE LOST CITY OF EXETER, Chips Barber
DIARY OF A DARTMOOR WALKER, Chips Barber
ADVENTURE THROUGH RED DEVON, R B Cattell
AN EXETER BOYHOOD, Frank Retter
UNDER SAIL THROUGH SOUTH DEVON, R B Cattell
IDE, Bill Rowland
DIARY OF A DEVONSHIRE WALKER, Chips Barber
RAMBLING IN PLYMOUTH, Woolley & Lister
GREAT LITTLE DARTMOOR BOOK, Chips Barber
GREAT LITTLE EXETER BOOK, Chips Barber
DEVONAIR BOOK OF FAMILY WALKS, Chips Barber
RUNNING IN DEVON, John Legge
MEMORIES OF NEWTON ABBOT, Elsie Townsend
CREDITON COLLECTION, Albert Labbett

HAUNTED HAPPENINGS IN DEVON, Judy Chard
MADE IN DEVON, Chips Barber & David FitzGerald
DARTMOOR IN COLOUR, Chips Barber
BURGH ISLAND AND BIGBURY BAY, Chips Barber & Judy Chard
DARK & DASTARDLY DARTMOOR, Sally and Chips Barber
TALKING ABOUT TOPSHAM, Sara Vernon
AN ALPHINGTON ALBUM, Pauline Aplin & Jeanne Gaskell
PICTURES OF PAIGNTON, Peter Tully
TALES OF THE UNEXPLAINED, Judy Chard
EXETER IN COLOUR, Chips Barber
TORBAY IN COLOUR, Chips Barber
THE TOTNES COLLECTION, Bill Bennett

First Published in 1989 by Obelisk Publications, 2 Church Hill, Pinhoe, Exeter, Devon
Designed by Chips Barber, Typset by Sally Barber
Printed in Great Britain by Penwell Ltd, Parkwood, Callington, Cornwall.
© Bernard Chapman 1989
All Rights Reserved

An early visitors' guide book to South East Devon says "Dawlish and Teignmouth are twin resorts between the Exe and Teign but they bear little resemblance! Dawlish is essentially pretty and petite - a gem among seaside resorts; the view obtained from the railway line of the lawn with houses on either side of its green expanse and divided down its centre by the docile Dawlish Water, suggests a dolls' house scene". Hopefully this little book will portray some of the other faces which Dawlish possesses.

Edwardian photographers may not have had very sophisticated equipment at their disposal but the sharpness of pictures like this take some matching even today! This view of the Marine Parade was taken about 1910 when the traffic was restricted to one doll's pram!

Looking the other way along the Marine Parade, the imposing building in the centre of the photo is the Public Baths which were built in 1830. Bathers had a choice of hot or cold, salt, freshwater, hip or shower baths. A large pump raised water from the sea. In 1895 the building was altered and became a gentlemen's club, and eventually a restaurant.

There are certain times when Dawlish's Marine Parade is a place to avoid, if possible. Here is such an occasion when a strong south easterly wind combines with a full tide to break with enormous ferocity against the sea wall. This photograph was taken in 1907 but similar scenes have been witnessed many times down the years.

This is the view that remains in the memory of most visitors to Dawlish who have enjoyed a stroll along the Marine Parade. This picture was taken about 1904 and although the view is still similar, there have been many changes. The iron footbridge over the railway was replaced by a concrete structure in 1965. The railway is just a single line and the complete absence of traffic must have created a very serene scene indeed.

Bathing machines existed on Dawlish beach until 1920 and possessed not only such essentials as pegs for hanging clothes and a seat on which to sit whilst changing, but also a carpet so that "the feet would not get chilled", an awning to screen the warmth of the sun's rays and even a footbath. Included in the modest hire fee was the facility to be pushed down to the water's edge by an attendant. This wonderful photograph of people at play dates back to 1911.

Coryton Cove was originally the gentlemen's bathing cove but by the time this photograph had been taken, in 1927, things had changed. The bathing huts no doubt provided good service to all the families visiting this popular cove. On the left hand side of the picture a small light railway can just be discerned. It was constructed so that materials could be taken from the main line track to fill a gap in the breakwater which was located at the western edge of this beach. Originally it had not been connected to the cliff and GWR decided that such a construction was needed to prevent beach erosion.

A vast number of Dawlishians can be seen here assembled on the main beach to await the start of a water polo game. The picture was taken about 1925 and a high proportion of the crowd wore something on their heads. The man in the centre foreground was Jack Lamacraft, owner of the largest local house building firm and member of the Dawlish Urban District Council.

Sea View House was demolished more than a century ago but this fine picture depicts its location at what today is known as Sea Lawn Terrace. Black Bridge and Langstone Cliff can be seen in the distance.

Dawlish has the rare distinction of having a main line railway line which runs right along its sea front. The route from Exeter was forged by Brunel in 1846 after many problems had been encountered along the estuary and around the coast line. Between Dawlish and Teignmouth there were originally six tunnels and they were Kennaway (200 yards), Coryton's (207 yards), Phillott's (48 yards), Clerk (52 yards), Parson's (at 374 yards the longest) and East Cliff, Teignmouth (320 yards). The Teignmouth tunnel was opened in 1884 and, because of cliff falls, Parson's was extended by 139 yards at the Dawlish end. This picture shows a steam train heading out of Dawlish and towards The Warren.

The first Dawlish Station was just a shed! It was open to the sun with a roof supported by iron stanchions yet despite its lack of substance looked like the station that exists at Starcross today. It was destroyed by fire on August 20 1873 and was replaced by a new one which was constructed of stone and opened in 1875. This view of the station was taken in 1908 and shows a healthy group of passengers waiting on the Exeter-bound platform.

Dawlish once boasted an important fishery with dozens of men employed as fishermen. If there was a large catch of herring Mr Tripe, of the Gresham Inn, acted as an agent for a London market. He would salt them in hampers together with layers of bracken and then dispatch them by the first available train. This photograph was taken at the turn of the century and shows large catches of fish.

This view was taken from the roof of the former Royal Hotel opposite the western end of the up platform in 1935. This photographic standpoint was one of the most popular because it provided a panoramic view of the red sandstone cliffs with their unusual formations. Seen here are The Parson and Clerk, Horse Rock, Old Maid Rock, Red Rock and Lea Mount.

Tennis being played on the Lawn - must be Lawn Tennis! This is how the game looked at Dawlish in about 1925. The flat grassland beside The Brook made it a wonderful venue and four courts provided visitors and locals with some rigorous exercise in beautiful, almost sub tropical surroundings.

More of the Lawn and surrounding area can be seen in this photograph which was taken in 1913. As we have come to expect the whole scene is neat, tidy and attractive. Enough to ensure that in the following decades Dawlish would thrive as a popular seaside resort sheltered by hills all around. The small weather station on the left foreground recorded the atmospheric conditions which were milder than almost every other resort in the Westcountry.

This wonderful photograph was taken about 1914 and shows that Dawlish, despite its benign climate, does at times suffer from a visitor called "Jack Frost". The frozen fountain provided a spectacle for the local population and enthusiastic photographers.

In 1962, almost half a century later, the icy hand of winter touched Dawlish again. An unusually prolonged cold spell meant that many homes in the town went without water for weeks, whilst the palm trees shivered beneath a coat of snow and ice.

Just look at how Piermont Place has changed through the years! This view was taken about 1938 and shows Hopkins and Sons' Garage which later became the site of Greenslades, the well known coach operator.

Many familiar landmarks can be readily identified on this aerial shot of Dawlish taken about 1930. The great number of awnings found in the shops along the Strand and Piermont Place clearly stand out as do the main bridges which span The Brook. Several well known local buildings seen here have been demolished, including St Mark's church and The Hut. This photo was taken by a photographer called Hobart who specialised in seaside town photography from the air. Probably the most telling sign that this photograph was taken well over half a century ago is the lack of traffic in and around the town.

This picture, taken in 1949, was a long way ahead of the days of a one way system in Dawlish. The streets of Dawlish were virtually deserted - you could park almost anywhere as this photograph demonstrates.

The expressions on the onlookers' faces are ones of pure joy as they behold some fun and frolicking in The Brook during the Queen Elizabeth II coronation celebrations in 1953. The Swimming Club and the Fire Service are indulging in some high jinks after a jet ball competition on The Lawn.

23

From fun and games to the problem of flooding. This scene occurred on 1 October 1960, a time when many towns and villages in Devon were inundated. This photograph was taken when a particularly high tide prevented The Brook's water from reaching the sea. The resulting flood spread over York Gardens and the surrounding streets.

On 4 May 1900 a public meeting was held in the Town Hall to discuss the possibility of staging a cart horse parade in Dawlish. A committee was formed and it was decided that the parade should take place on Whit Monday. It was open to entrants within a 5 mile radius in order to allow rivals from Teignmouth to take part. Our photo shows one of the many parades staged, this one probably being 1910. The arrival of the motor car heralded a gradual decline in the number of horses and the event thus succumbed to the machine age.

It was common practice to say whose inn it actually was and in this 1908 photo of Beach Lane you can see "Manning's Exeter Inn" (previously Wheeler's) and "Eveleigh's Railway Inn" (previously Mitchell's). The shop in the foreground later became Bill Dart's fish shop. A century ago Dawlish had 14 pubs and only one bank, the town obviously was more concerned with liquid assets!

26

A keen eye will detect the familiar name of W H Smith and Son in the centre of this photograph of The Strand taken in 1908. The famous stationers later moved to Piermont Place. On the right hand side is Shapter's, then an ironmongery shop, later a garage and now Gateway supermarket.

The Bartons contain some elegant houses and in this photograph of 1906 stand in an almost traffic-free road. The three storey house standing next to the Parish Church was badly damaged by fire in 1913. The site is now occupied by the war memorial.

This is what the corner of Park Road and Regent Street looked like about 1910. The small former West End Post Office stands as a most distinct landmark.

29

In 1908 the taking of a photograph was not a common practice and people were naturally curious. Here they have turned out in force to pose for this photograph in Hatcher Street - a wonderful period piece!

By contrast the menfolk in this Hatcher Street photograph of about 1933 are captured for posterity whilst engaged in the arduous task of hauling electric cables uphill to link them with pylons taking power to nearby Ashcombe and Starcross. Electricity was generated in a works in Brook Street from 1910 but after 1929 a change of ownership and policy led to the town receiving its power from Newton Abbot. The 'giant' in the foreground was 'Long Tom' Richards.

Regular customers to "Dawlish News" in Queen Street will no doubt find this picture a most fascinating one to study for it clearly shows their newsagency as it was in 1908.

The gardens in front of these properties in Queen Street disappeared in 1965 when the street was widened. This lovely view taken looking down the hill was captured in 1908. The house at the bottom of the hill later became The Scala Cinema, the manager being the famous Charlie Payne.

This photograph of Brook Street was taken more than 80 years ago which makes even the youngest person in the scene a very senior citizen. The Manor Inn is no longer a pub! In the 1930s most of Brook Street was condemned as being unfit for human habitation. Today many of the houses are fetching high prices as 'desirable residences'.

The other end of Brook Street! How many of the children can you spot from the photograph opposite?

35

Alexandra Place in 1908. The railings around the gardens were taken during World War II to 'make guns to defeat Hitler'.

There have not been too many changes to this view of West Cliff since it was taken several decades ago. However, Dawlish's population has grown steadily since the turn of the century. When this photograph was taken the town had about 5,000 residents. Today the population is more than double that number!

Old Town Street.
38

Old Town Street was a much quieter road in 1908 apart from the occasional horse and trap.

The cottages in the foreground of this 1908 photo have now disappeared leaving a pleasant empty space with public telephone and seat. During World War II the site was occupied by an air raid shelter.

The Haldon Harriers met frequently in the winter months of the early 1900s. The hounds were brought from Kingsteignton by Mr Hepper. As a rule the hunt went off in a north easterly direction and it was not uncommon for a stop to he made at Langdon Farm where the owner, Mr Carell Adams, supplied refreshments for both man and beast. Here they can be seen outside the London Hotel in 1909 which is now occupied by Woolworth's.

The Pleasant Sunday Hour Orchestra played light classics in The Hut, seen behind them, for many years and included many well known local musicians, such as Janny Gibbings, Sonny Cridge and Will Pike. This photograph was taken about 1935 some four years before the orchestra was disbanded.

Coronation Tea Party in The Hut. Many Dawlish folk will know at least one person in this picture taken at the celebrated venue of The Hut. Each child had a souvenir Coronation mug and most wore a paper hat. The Hut was the social centre of Dawlish for many years. It started life in Sutton Viney as a canteen for the Australian army. It was obtained for Dawlish by Charlie Ross who intended it to be an entertainments centre and was opened on 16 December 1920. It served the town well for numerous functions until 1959 when its condition had become so dangerous that it had to be demolished. Its site on Barton Hill is now a car park.

The people of Dawlish have always been keen thespians! Here are some of the stars of the 1936 production, by the Dawlish Pantomime Company, of "Robinson Crusoe". The first panto was performed in The Hut in 1934 and was so popular that it became an annual institution. The profits were given to charities. Nan Sampson, so often the principal boy, was a leading light in the movement and after 1938 was the sole promoter of the company. In 1940 she had to cancel the show, at short notice, because her co-producer and principal comedian, Sid Vernon, received his calling up papers. "Cinderella" was thus delayed for six years until it was played to record audiences in 1946!

They may have been simply "Babes in the Wood" in 1953 but most of the cast of this pantomime are much older and wiser today!

45

In November 1960 a party was given to celebrate the 50th production by the Repertory company. By this time the company had attracted a healthy membership who can be seen enjoying this auspicious occasion. Photos of previous productions can be seen displayed on the walls. Sid Thorpe who was Dawlish's best known character is seen in the foreground wearing white trousers and shirt.

The next two photographs depict the floral dance which performed through the streets of Dawlish on 2 June 1953 which is better remembered as Coronation Day! Probably no other town in Devon made as enthusiastic an effort to celebrate such an historic occasion. The day began with pensioners of the Royal Navy firing a gun salute at 6.00 am and this signalled the start of a 5 mile race in which 8 cyclists hurtled around the Lawn. Other events followed.

47

There was a sports day for children but a sharp downpour resulted in around 1,250 children being fed in various halls throughout the town instead of on The Lawn. But the fun and games went on with Des Tickell, R Gibbings and T Shorland climbing the greasy pole whilst Mrs Townsend, Miss Castle and Mrs Ellacott indulged in a pillow fight. Two celebratory fires were lit. One was on the beach where a miniature Spanish Galleon was set alight and the other was a bonfire on top of Langstone Cliff, just one of a chain of over 2,000 such fires set up by boy scout troops all around the coastline.

48

Street parties were the order of the day for the Coronation and scenes like this were common all over the country. Here the children of Brook Street can be seen in festive mood with their parents and grandparents supervising.

Albert Place or is it Albert Plaice? The Dawlish folk have every reason to be cheerful as this is a victory tea to celebrate the end of World War II. Various parades and celebrations took place all over the kingdom. Here, outside Haywood's Fish and Chip Shop, now the laundrette, are many children who grew up in the hard times between 1939 and 1945.

In June 1961 the choir of the Parish Church posed for this photograph which captures many little angelic smiles!

51

These are the ladies who made up the Dawlish Girls' School staff in 1934. They were (back L to R) Miss Flynn, Miss Hinton, Miss Wooley, Miss Cox, (front L to R) Mrs Rowley, Miss Richards and Miss Wilkinson who later became Mrs Williams.

The Dawlish Boys' School staff of 1934 which included (back L to R) Hedley Hoare, Eric Fountain, (front L to R) Jack Shobrook, George Lamacraft and Brian Crispin.

53

As we have already seen, Dawlish really entered into the spirit of things to celebrate the Coronation. The Oakhill Blonde Bombshells met the Newlands and St Mary's Wildcats in a ladies' football match on The Lawn. The latter won an exciting game by 2 goals to 1. The real losers were the match officials who raced for safety but were captured and thrown into The Brook. Bill Cheetham avenged Frank Bolt's soaking by entering the ladies' dressing room and piled up all the 22 players' clothes into a single heap on the floor!

In 1965 the Dawlish 1st XI were the proud winners of the East Devon Senior Cup.

By 1897, when this photograph was taken, Newberrys had well and truly established themselves as carriers operating in South Devon. They had started in the late eighteenth century with a team of packhorses, and to travel between Dawlish and Exeter they used an inland route over Haldon via Chudleigh as the coastal route was too marshy. As Dawlish grew a new service was opened to Teignmouth. In addition to carting goods Newberrys also became involved in the furniture removal business. One less pleasant task was that of conveying the paupers of Dawlish to the dreaded workhouse.

Members of the Dawlish Urban District Council at the Manor in 1963.

These vigilant men comprised the Dawlish Fire Brigade of 1940, photographed outside the old fire station at Barton Hill. The men in the back row are seated on the Dawlish fire engine, 'Sir Redvers Buller'. They were the regular firemen. Those standing were recruited for the war-time 'Auxiliary Fire Service'. Their equipment consisted of two pumps which could be towed by private cars.

Holcombe was a much quieter village when this photograph was taken at the turn of the century. The single street descended the hillside below the Castle Inn and wound its way up the opposite side of the valley towards Teignmouth. Pretty thatched cottages and gardens edged both sides of the road and just beyond this, farmers' fields ran almost right down to the road.

It is never easy trying to take photographs from an aeroplane and this effort taken about 1927 lacks in quality. However it reveals Dawlish before it started spreading outwards towards Starcross and many hundreds of Dawlish people now live in houses built on the fields shown in this picture.

February 19 1935 was the date for the laying of the foundation stone for the first house on the Marina Estate. Here Mr Jack Lamacraft can be seen performing the ceremony. The council had bought the Pidgley estate with the intention of developing it for housing and sports facilities. Firmly at the back of their mind was the job opportunities it created because unemployment was high in the town and this project gave work to 30 men who would have otherwise been unemployed. Following the ceremony the dignitaries repaired to the Grand Hotel for a celebration lunch.

The 35th birthday of the Dawlish Townswomen's Guild was celebrated at the Langstone Cliff Hotel in May 1966. A careful look at this select group *of ladies will reveal a high proportion of the most noted female personalities of Dawlish. Can you spot the odd one out?*

Just before the Second World War Piermont Place looked just like this. However it's one place you wouldn't have bought this book as those well known booksellers left the town many years ago. We hope you enjoyed meeting many old but familiar places and faces and we hope that we will be able to feature many more in future editions. Thank you for your support.